Handy Georgia Genealogy Handbook

I0450524

By Gary L. Morris

ISBN-13: 978-1506190105

ISBN-10: 1506190103

Table of Contents

Notes

Genealogical Research in Georgia

Georgia has a long and colorful history, making it an ideal state in which to conduct research. There are many historical and genealogical records available for Georgia but you won't have to dig too much for them; we'll show you exactly where they are. To get you started in tracing your Georgia ancestry, we'll introduce you to those records, and help you to understand:

1. What they are
2. Where to find them
3. How to use them

These records can be found both online and off, so we'll introduce you to online websites, indexes and databases, as well as brick-and-mortar repositories and other institutions that will help with your research in Georgia. So that you will have a more comprehensive understanding of these records, we have provided a brief history of the "Peach State" to illustrate what type of records may have been generated during specific time periods. That information will assist you in pinpointing times and locations on which to focus the search for your Georgia ancestors and their records.

A Brief History of Georgia

There is definitely nothing "brief" about Georgia's history, but here we shall stick to that which is genealogically relevant. For a more in-depth overview of Georgia's history, visit the **New Georgia Encyclopaedia**.

New Georgia Encyclopaedia link to:
http://www.georgiaencyclopedia.org/articles/history-archaeology/georgia-history-overview

Spanish explorers roamed through the area of modern day Georgia from the mid 16th century up until around 1660. Although Spanish missionaries established missions which were designed to assimilate the Native Indian population into the colonial system, it was the British who initially colonized the region. English settlers began arriving from South Carolina during the mid 17th century, and they established a thriving slave trade of the Native American Indians, as well as a profitable trade in deer skins.

Savannah was the first settlement established by the British in 1733. It was run much differently from the other British colonies, being governed by a Board of Trustees which was based in England. It was also different in that it was the only colony in which slavery was banned, and additionally the colony disallowed rum, lawyers and Catholics. As the youngest colony with the smallest population, shortest colonial experience, and least development, Georgia remained very much on the periphery of Revolutionary War politics and wartime action.

Georgia lifted the ban on slavery in 1749 and became a Royal colony in 1752. Georgia was well represented at the Second Continental Congress and three Georgians signed the Declaration of Independence, and a further two signing the new US Constitution at the Constitutional Convention in 1787. Georgia became the fourth state to enter the Union upon ratifying the Constitution on January 2, 1788.

Georgia was always home to a significant population of Native Americans, and it stayed as such for longer than most other states. The Cherokees were among the most well known tribes, and their forced exile known as the "Trail of Tears" when they were removed from the northwest part of the territory is a potent symbol of the tragedy of all such removals. Georgia's development was accelerated by the construction of the Augusta, Athens, Savannah, and Macon railways during the 1830's and when Atlanta (initially named Terminus) was established in 1837, the state was well on its way to becoming a formidable economic and political power.

Important Genealogical Dates in Georgia History

- **1733** – Savannah established

- **1734** – Effingham County area settled by German Protestant refugees from Salzburg

- **1742** – Battle of Bloody Marsh

- **1749** – Slavery legalized

- **1752** – Becomes a Royal Colony

- **1758** – Divided into twelve parishes

- **1777** – Twelve parishes divided into seven colonies

- **1778** – British troops occupy Savannah

- **1838** – Cherokee Indians removed from Georgia

- **1861** – Secedes from Union

- **1864** – Union army captures Savannah and Atlanta

- **1870** – Readmitted to Union

Famous Battles Fought in Georgia

Georgia was a strategic area during the Civil War, and the region saw much action. There were over 500 skirmishes in Georgia, so here we present only the major battles. If you wish to view a more extensive listing, you can visit the **National Park Service** website. The battle accounts can be very effective in uncovering the military records of your ancestor. They can tell you what regiments fought in which battles, and often include the names and ranks of many officers and enlisted men. Following are the most famous battles fought in Georgia and links to useful information about them.

Battle of Chickamauga -1863
Battle of Chickamauga:
http://www.civilwar.org/battlefields/chickamauga.html

Battle of Kennesaw Mountain – 1864
Battle of Kennesaw Mountain:
http://www.civilwar.org/battlefields/kennesaw-mountain.html

The Battle of Peachtree Creek – 1864
The Battle of Peachtree Creek: http://www.historynet.com/battle-of-peachtree-creek.htm

Battle of Atlanta – 1864
Battle of Atlanta: http://www.historynet.com/battle-of-atlanta

National Park Service:
http://georgiainfo.galileo.usg.edu/cwbattle.htm

Colonial Georgia Genealogical Records

The Colonial era is a very important genealogical stepping-stone for researching your Georgia ancestry, especially if your ancestor was an early settler. An excellent website to view Colonial era records is the **Georgia Pioneers** website. It was developed by Jeannette Holland Austin and contains traced genealogies, probate records, ship's passenger lists, confederate deaths, revolutionary war pensions, obituaries, marriages, cemeteries, census, Cherokee records, births, school records, land grants and more.

Georgia Pioneers:
http://www.georgiapioneers.com/content/colonialexplan.html

The **Middle Georgia Regional Library** - has an extensive collection of Colonial records from the original thirteen colonies recognized as one of the finest of such collections available.

1180 Washington Ave,
Macon, GA 31201
Tel: 478-744-0800

Middle Georgia Regional Library:
http://www.co.bibb.ga.us/library/gh.htm

Common Georgia Genealogical Issues and Resources to Overcome Them

Boundary Changes: Boundary changes are a common obstacle when researching Georgia ancestors. You could be searching for an ancestor's record in one county when in fact it is stored in a different one due to historical county boundary changes. The **Atlas of Historical County Boundaries** can help you to overcome that problem. It provides a chronological listing of every boundary change that has occurred in the history of Georgia.

Atlas of Historical County Boundaries:
http://publications.newberry.org/ahcbp/documents/GA_Consolidated _Chronology.htm#Consolidated_Chronology

Name Changes: Surname changes, variations, and misspellings can complicate genealogical research. It is important to check all spelling variations. Soundex, a program that indexes names by sound, is a useful first step, but you can't rely on it completely as some name variations result in different Soundex codes. The surnames could be different, but the first name may be different too. You can also find records filed under initials, middle names, and nicknames as well, so you will need to **get creative with surname variations** and spellings in order to cover all the possibilities. For help with surname variations read our instructional article on **How to Use Soundex**.

get creative with surname variations:
http://obituarieshelp.org/blog/?p=634

How to Use Soundex link to: http://obituarieshelp.org/blog/?p=505

Georgia Genealogical Organizations and Archives

Genealogical resources include not only records, but the organizations that house them, or can direct you to them. These institutions include: *Archives, Libraries, Genealogical Societies, Family History Centers, Universities, Churches, and Museums.*

Following are links to their websites, their physical addresses, and a summary of the records you can find there.

Georgia Archives

Georgia State Archives and Libraries – vital records, land records, census records, Native and African American records, death certificates

5800 Jonesboro Road
Morrow, GA 30260
Tel: 678.364.3710

Georgia State Archives and Libraries:
http://www.georgiaarchives.org/

National Archives at Atlanta – census records, land records, military records, passenger lists, immigration and naturalization records, Native and African American records

5780 Jonesboro Road
Morrow, Georgia 30260
Tel: 770-968-2100
Fax: 770-968-2547
Email:atlanta.archives@nara.gov

National Archives at Atlanta:
http://www.archives.gov/research/genealogy/index.html

Georgia State University Library Archives – manuscripts, organizational records, historical photographs, rare books, women's movement records

Special Collections & Archives
Georgia State University Library
100 Decatur Street, SE
Atlanta, Georgia 30303-3202
Tel: 404- 413-2880
Fax: 404- 413-2881
E-Mail: archives@gsu.edu

Georgia State University Library Archives:
http://library.gsu.edu/417.html

Dougherty County Public Library – death indexes, census records, divorce index, marriage records, slave schedules, passenger lists, military records and more

Central Branch 3rd floor
300 Pine Ave. Albany, GA

Dougherty County Public Library:
http://www.swggs.org/resources.html

Georgia Genealogical and Historical Societies

Genealogical and historical societies have access to extensive catalogues of genealogical data. They are also able to offer expert guidance for genealogical researchers. Many members are professional genealogists who are most willing to share their expertise in finding ancestors.

Georgia Genealogical Society – naturalization records index, land records transcripts, clerk's records

P.O. Box 550247
Atlanta, GA 30355-2747

Georgia Genealogical Society: http://www.gagensociety.org/

Georgia Historical Society – miscellaneous genealogical and historical resources

SAVANNAH HEADQUARTERS

501 Whitaker Street
Savannah, GA 31401
Tel: 912.651.2125
Fax: 912.651.2831

ATLANTA OFFICE

260 14th Street, N.W., Suite A-148
Atlanta, GA 30318
Tel: 404.382.5410
Fax: 404.671.8570

Georgia Historical Society: http://georgiahistory.com/

Augusta Genealogical Society – miscellaneous resources including naturalization records index, probate records, estate records, marriage indexes, and death index

P.O. Box 3743
Augusta 30914-3743

Augusta Genealogical Society: http://augustagensociety.org/

East Georgia Genealogical Society – cemetery records, wills, family bibles, tax lists, and other genealogical resources

P.O. Box 117
Winder, GA 30680

East Georgia Genealogical Society:
http://www.rootsweb.ancestry.com/~gaeggs/

Central Georgia Genealogical Society – cemetery records, historical photographs, and other resources

Central Georgia Genealogical Society link to:
http://www.cggs.org/

Georgia Family History Centers

The Family History Centers run by the LDS Church offer free access to billions of genealogical records for free to the general public. They also provide classes on genealogy and one-on-one assistance to inexperienced family historians. Here you will find a **Complete Listing of Georgia Family History Centers**.

Complete Listing of Georgia Family History Centers:
https://familysearch.org/locations/centerlocator

Georgia Mailing Lists

Mailing lists are internet based facilities that use email to distribute a single message to all who subscribe to it. When information on a particular surname, new records, or any other important genealogy information related to the mailing list topic becomes available, the subscribers are alerted to it. Joining a mailing list is an excellent way to stay up to date on Georgia genealogy research topics. Rootsweb have an extensive listing of **Georgia Mailing Lists** on a variety of topics.

Georgia Mailing Lists:
http://lists.rootsweb.ancestry.com/index/usa/GA/misc.html

Georgia Message Boards

A message board is another internet based facility where people can post questions about a specific genealogy topic and have it answered by other genealogists. If you have questions about a surname, record type, or research topic, you can post your question and other researchers and genealogists will help you with the answer. Be sure to check back regularly, as the answers are not emailed to you. The Georgia Message Boards at **Rootsweb** are completely free to use.

Rootsweb:
http://boards.rootsweb.com/localities.northam.usa.states/mb.ashx

Georgia Newspapers and Periodicals

Many genealogy periodicals and historical newspapers contain reprinted copies of family genealogies, transcripts of family Bible records, information about local records and archives, census indexes, church records, queries, land records, obituaries, court records, cemetery records, and wills. The following sites have historical Georgia newspapers and periodicals that you can search online or on-site.

Digital Library of Georgia – excellent collection of historical newspapers for Georgia dating from the 19th century

Digital Library of Georgia:
http://dlg.galileo.usg.edu/MediaTypes/Newspapers.html

University of Georgia Libraries – Georgia Newspaper Project – catalog of historical Georgia newspapers dating from the 18th century

University of Georgia Libraries: http://www.libs.uga.edu/gnp/

The Online Books Page – links to historical books and periodicals available for viewing online, dating from mid-16th century

The Online Books Page:
http://onlinebooks.library.upenn.edu/webbin/book//browse?type=lcs ubc&key=Georgia%20--%20History%20--%20Periodicals

NewspaperArchive.com – largest online database of historical newspapers in the world.

NewspaperArchive.com link to: http://newspaperarchive.com/

<u>Historical Georgia Maps and Gazetteers</u>

Maps are an integral part of genealogical research. They help us to locate landmarks, towns, cities, parishes, states, provinces, waterways and roads and streets. They also help us to determine when and where boundary changes might have taken place, and give us a visualization of the area we're researching in. For locating place names, a gazetteer is the best possible resource for any genealogist. Gazetteers are also sometimes called "place name dictionaries", and can help you to locate the area in which you need to conduct research. Below are links to the maps and gazetteers for research in Georgia.

Peabody GNIS Service – Georgia: http://peabody.research.yale.edu/cgi-bin/Query.GNIS?ST=Georgia&SU=1

Color Landform Atlas – Georgia: http://fermi.jhuapl.edu/states/ga_0.html

1985 U.S. Atlas: http://www.livgenmi.com/1895/GA/

Georgia Hometown Locator: http://georgia.hometownlocator.com/

Georgia City Directories

City directories are similar to telephone directories in that they list the residents of a particular area. The difference though is what is important to genealogists, and that is they pre-date telephone directories. You can find an ancestor's information such as their street address, place of employment, occupation, or the name of their spouse. A one-stop-shop for finding city directories in Georgia is the **Georgia Online Historical Directories** which contains a listing of every available city and historical directory related to Georgia.

Georgia Online Historical Directories :
https://sites.google.com/site/onlinedirectorysite/Home/usa/ga

University of Georgia Libraries – City directories dating from mid nineteenth century for hundreds of cities in Georgia

University of Georgia Libraries:
http://www.libs.uga.edu/magil/collections/citydirectories.html

Atlanta-Fulton Public Library System - Atlanta City Directories from 1867, Atlanta Telephone Directories from 1946 and Criss-Cross Directories from 1946

Atlanta-Fulton Public Library System:
http://www.afpls.org/special-collections-m

Georgia Genealogical Records

<u>Birth, Death, Marriage and Divorce Records</u> – Also known as vital records, birth, death, and marriage certificates are the most basic, yet most important records attached to your ancestor. The reason for their importance is that they not only place your ancestor in a specific place at a definite time, but potentially connect the individual to other relatives. Below is a list of repositories and websites where you can find Georgia vital records

Georgia Department of Public Health Vital Records – birth, death, marriage and divorce records from 1919 to present

2600 Skyland Drive
NE Atlanta, GA 30319-3640

Georgia Department of Public Health Vital Records:
http://www.cdc.gov/nchs/w2w/georgia.htm

Rootsweb Georgia Databases – searchable online marriage and death indexes contributed by other family historians

Rootsweb Georgia Databases:
http://userdb.rootsweb.ancestry.com/regional.html#Georgia

Ancestry.com (requires payment) – **Georgia Marriages 1699-1944**

Georgia Marriages 1699-1944:
http://search.ancestry.com/search/db.aspx?dbid=7839&cj=1&netid=cj&o_xid=0000584978&o_lid=0000584978&o_sch=Affiliate+External

Georgia, Births, and Christenings, 1754-1960 - index to birth, baptism, and christening records from Georgia

Georgia, Births, and Christenings, 1754-1960:
https://familysearch.org/search/collection/1674802

Atlanta Birth Records from **1887** can be found at:

Fulton County Health Department
141 Prior Street
Atlanta, GA 30303
Tel: 404-730-4000

Fulton County Health Department:
http://www.fultoncountyga.gov/dhw-vital-records

Savannah Birth Records dating from **1890** to the present are
available from:

Chatham County Health Department
2011 Eisenhower Drive
P.O. Box 14257
Savannah, GA 31406
Tel: 912-356-2441

Chatham County Health Department: http://www.gachd.org/

Census Reports

Census records are among the most important genealogical documents for placing your ancestor in a particular place at a specific time. Like BDM records, they can also lead you to other ancestors, particularly those who were living under the authority of the head of household.

Georgia census records are available from 1790-1930, and there are several repositories, both online and off, where you can find them.

Census-Online – online Georgia census reports from 1790-1930

Census-Online: http://www.census-online.com/links/GA/1790.html

National Archives at Atlanta – Georgia census records from 1820-1930

5780 Jonesboro Road
Morrow, Georgia 30260
Tel: 770-968-2100
Fax: 770-968-2547
Email:atlanta.archives@nara.gov

National Archives at Atlanta:
http://www.archives.gov/research/genealogy/index.html

Access Genealogy - Georgia census records from 1820-1930

Access Genealogy:
http://www.accessgenealogy.com/census/georgia-census-records.htm

African American Census Schedules Online – slave schedules, mortality schedules, slave-owners census

African American Census Schedules Online:
http://www.afrigeneas.com/aacensus/ga/

Native Americans in Census Records (US National Archives)

Native Americans in Census Records:
http://www.archives.gov/research/census/native-americans/

Georgia Church Records

Church and synagogue records are a valuable resource, especially for baptisms, marriages, and burials that took place before 1900. You will need to at least have an idea of your ancestor's religious denomination, and in most cases you will have to visit a brick and mortar establishment to view them.

Most church records are kept by the individual church, although in some denominations, records are placed in a regional archive or maintained at the diocesan level. Local Historical Societies are sometimes the repository for the state's older church records. Below are links archives that maintain church records, as well as a few databases that can be viewed online.

The **Family History Library** contains many church records from a variety of denominations on microfilm.

Family History Library:
http://familysearch.org/learn/wiki/en/Family_History_Library

Georgia State Archives – microfilmed church records of the following denominations; A.M.E. (African Methodist Episcopal), Baptist, Catholic, Christian, Church of Christ, Church of God, Congregational, Disciples of Christ, Episcopal, Lutheran, Methodist, Presbyterian, Primative Baptist, Quaker, Synagogues, United Brethren in Christ

Georgia State Archives:
http://cdm.georgiaarchives.org:2011/cdm/landingpage/collection/churchcards

Mercer University Library – historical Baptist record collection

1300 Edgewood Avenue
Macon, GA 31207
Tel: 478- 301-2961
Fax: 478- 301-2252

Mercer University Library:
http://libraries.mercer.edu/tarver/archives/special-collections-baptist-university-archives/media/ChurchRecords.pdf

Central Repositories for Denominational Records

Most of the records of individual denominations are kept in central repositories. Below is a list of the major congregational archives in Georgia with links to their websites, physical addresses, and contact information.

Methodist

Methodist Archives

P.O. Box 24081
St. Simons Island, GA 31522
Tel: (912) 638-4050
Fax: (912) 638-9050
Email: methmuse@bellsouth.net

Methodist Archives:
http://www.gcah.org/site/c.ghKJI0PHIoE/b.2901109/k.12B1/Researching_Your_United_Methodist_Ancestors.htm

Moravian

The Moravian Archives
41 West Locust Street
Bethlehem, Pennsylvania 18018
United States of America
Tel: (610) 866-3255
Fax: (610) 866-9210

The Moravian Archives:
http://www.moravianchurcharchives.org/general.php

Roman Catholic

Archdiocese of Atlanta
680 W. Peachtree Street, N.W.
Atlanta, GA 30308-1984
Tel: (404) 978-2772
Fax: (404) 885-7462

Archdiocese of Atlanta: http://www.archatl.com/

Catholic Diocese of Savannah
601 East Liberty St.
Savannah, GA 31401
Tel: (912) 201-4070

Catholic Diocese of Savannah: http://diosav.org/node/205

Georgia Military Records

More than 40 million Americans have participated in some time of war service since America was colonized. The chance of finding your ancestor amongst those records is exceptionally high. Military records can even reveal individuals who never actually served, such as those who registered for the two World Wars but were never called to duty.

Below are a number of links to websites and archives that contain Georgia military records.

Georgia Archives – Confederate enlistment oaths and discharge files, Confederate Pension Applications 1879-1960, confederate Pension Application supplements, militia enrolment lists 1864, Spanish American War Service Summation Cards,

Georgia Archives: http://cdm.georgiaarchives.org:2011/cdm/

U.S. National Archives – WWI Draft registration cards, casualties lists, WWI and WWII service records, Korean War records, Vietnam War records, Civil War and Spanish-American War records, and casualties lists.

U.S. National Archives: http://www.archives.gov/research/military/veterans/online.html

US Department of Veterans Affairs Nationwide Gravesite Locator – includes information on veterans and their family members buried in veterans and military cemeteries having a government grave marker.

US Department of Veterans Affairs Nationwide Gravesite Locator: http://gravelocator.cem.va.gov/

United States Index to Indian Wars Pension Files, 1892-1926 – military pension records of soldiers who fought in the Indian Wars between 1817 and 1898

United States Index to Indian Wars Pension Files, 1892-1926: https://familysearch.org/search/collection/1979427

United States Mexican War Pension Index, 1887-1926 - index to Mexican War pension files for service between 1846 and 1848

United States Mexican War Pension Index, 1887-1926: https://familysearch.org/search/collection/1979390

Civil War Soldiers Service Records - Service records for both Union and Confederate soldiers indexed by soldier's name, rank, and unit.

Civil War Soldier Service Records: http://go.fold3.com/civilwar_records/

Georgia Cemetery Records

As convenient as it is to search cemetery records online, keep in mind that there are a few disadvantages over visiting a cemetery in person. They are:

- Tombstone information is not always accurately transcribed
- The arrangement of the graves in a cemetery can be crucial as family members are often buried next to each other or in the same grave. This arrangement is not always preserved in the alphabetical indexes that are found online.

With that information in mind, the following websites have databases that can be searched online for Georgia Cemetery records.

Georgia Tombstone Transcription Project - death and burial records

Georgia Tombstone Transcription Project:
http://www.usgwtombstones.org/georgia/georgia.html

African American Cemeteries Online – African American, slave, and Native American cemetery records

African American Cemeteries Online:
http://africanamericancemeteries.com/ar/

Access Genealogy – huge database of Georgia cemetery record transcriptions

Access Genealogy:
http://www.accessgenealogy.com/cemetery/georgia-cemetery-records.htm

Find a Grave – over 100 million grave records can be searched on this site. Search can be conducted by name, location, or cemetery name.

Find a Grave: http://www.findagrave.com/

Interment.net - A free online database containing approximately 4 million cemetery records from around the world.

Interment.net: **http://www.interment.net/**

Billion Graves – as the name implies, you can search a billion records including headstone photos, transcriptions, cemetery records, and grave locations.

Billion Graves:
http://billiongraves.com/pages/search/index.php#cemetery

Georgia Obituaries

Obituaries can reveal a wealth about our ancestor and other relatives. You can search our **Georgia Newspaper Obituaries Listings** from hundreds of Georgia newspapers online for free.

Georgia Newspaper Obituaries Listings:
http://obituarieshelp.org/georgia_newspaper_obituaries.html

Georgia Wills and Probate Records

The documents found in a probate packet may include a complete inventory of a person's estate, newspaper entries, witness testimony, a copy of a will, list of debtors and creditors, names of executors or trustees, names of heirs. They can not only tell you about the ancestor you're currently researching, but lead to other ancestors. Most of these records must be accessed at a county court or clerk's office, but some can be found online as well. You can obtain copies of the original probate records by writing to the county clerk.

Digital Images of Clarke County, Georgia Wills and Estates – wills abstracts, probate records, estate records, tax books

Digital Images of Clarke County, Georgia Wills and Estates: http://genealogy-georgiapioneers.blogspot.de/

Georgia State Archives and Libraries – Chatham County Deed Books, Superior Court records, Colonial Will Books, Colonial Wills, County records

5800 Jonesboro Road
Morrow, GA 30260
Tel: 678.364.3710

Georgia State Archives and Libraries: http://cdm.georgiaarchives.org:2011/cdm/

Georgia Immigration and Naturalization Records

The naturalization process generated many types of records, including petitions, declarations of intention, and oaths of allegiance. These records can provide family historians with information such as a person's birth date and place of birth, immigration year, marital status, spouse information, occupation, witnesses' names and addresses, and more.

US National Archives – Immigration and Naturalization records for the entire United States

US National Archives:
http://www.archives.gov/research/immigration/passenger-arrival.html

Family Search – naturalizations and citizenship records dating from 1789

Family Search:
https://familysearch.org/search/catalog/results#count=20&query=%2Bsubject_id%3A505381

Georgia Native American Records

Georgia State Archives and Libraries – vital records, land records, census records, Native and African American records, death certificates

5800 Jonesboro Road
Morrow, GA 30260
Tel: 678.364.3710

Georgia State Archives and Libraries:
http://www.georgiaarchives.org/

East Georgia Genealogical Society – cemetery records, wills, family bibles, tax lists, and other genealogical resources

P.O. Box 117
Winder, GA 30680

East Georgia Genealogical Society:
http://www.rootsweb.ancestry.com/~gaeggs/

Access Genealogy – Georgia Native American census records, tribal histories, and much more

Access Genealogy:
http://www.accessgenealogy.com/native/georgia-indian-tribes.htm

Bureau of Indian Affairs

Bureau of Indian Affairs: http://www.bia.gov/

Missing Matriarchs – Resources for Researching Female Georgia Ancestors

Looking for female ancestors requires an adjustment of how we view traditional records sources. A woman's identity was often under that of her husband, and often individual records for them can be difficult to locate. The following resources are effective in locating female ancestors in Georgia where traditional records may not reveal them.

Marriage and Divorce Records

Counties started recording marriages in 1785. Those records are kept by the county court clerk or the clerk of the county Ordinary court. Between 1785 and 1835, divorces were overseen by the Georgia State Legislature. After 1835 jurisdiction over divorces was given to the county Superior courts. Early county records that have been microfilmed are:

1. Baker County Court of Ordinary marriage records, 1874-1935 (film 0522798 ff.) – Baker County Courthouse in Newton
2. Baker County Superior Court minutes. 1879-1914 (film 0522793 ff.) - Baker County Courthouse in Newton
3. Effingham County Court of marriage records and miscellaneous records, 1791-1943 (film 0180394 ff.) and marriage index, 1790-1935 (film 0180393 ff.) – Effingham County Courthouse un Springfield
4. Effingham County Superior Court minutes, 1821-1901 (film 0180383 ff.) - Effingham County Courthouse in Springfield

Bibliographies

- *Ambiguous Lives: Free Women of Color in Rural Georgia, 1789-1879,* Adele Logan Alexander (Little Rock University of Arkansas Press, 1991)
- *Status of Women in Georgia, 1783-1860,* Eleanor Miwot Boatwright (Carlson Publishing, 1994)
- *The Georgians: Genealogies of Pioneer Settlers,* Jeanette Holland Austin (Genealogical Publishing Company, 19840
- *A List of the Early Settlers of Georgia,* E.Merton Coulter and Albert B. Saye (Baltimore Clearfield Company, 1998)
- *Southern Comfort: Quilts from the Atlanta Historical Society,* (Atlanta Historical Society, 1978)

Selected Resources for Georgia Women's History

Special Collections & Archives
Georgia State University Library
100 Decatur Street, SE
Atlanta, Georgia 30303-3202
Tel: 404- 413-2880
Fax: 404- 413-2881
E-Mail: archives@gsu.edu

Southern Association of Women Historians
Department of History
Agnes Scott College
Decatur, GA 33030-3797

Common Georgia Surnames

The following surnames are among the most common in Georgia and are also being currently researched by other genealogists. If you find your surname here, there is a chance that some research has already been performed on your ancestor.

Appling, Banks, Baker, Bartow, Berrien, Baldwin, Bibb, Brooks, Bryan, Bulloch, Burke, Butts, Camden, Campbell, Carroll, Cass, Catoosa, Charlton, Chatham, Chattooga, Chattahoochee, Cherokee, Clarke, Clay, Clayton, Clinch, Cobb, Coffee, Columbia, Coweta, Crawford, Dade, Dawson, Decatur, Dekalb, Dodge, Dooly, Dougherty, Douglas, Early, Echols, Effingham, Elbert, Emanuel, Fannin, Fayette,| Floyd, Forsyth, Franklin, Fulton, Gilmer, Glascock, Glynn, Greene, Gwinnett, Habersham, Hall, Hancock, Haralson, Harris, Hart,| Heard, Henry, Houston, Irwin, Jackson, Jasper, Jefferson, Johnson, Jones, Laurens, Lee, Liberty, Lincoln, Lowndes, Macon, Madison, Marion, McDuffie, McIntosh, Meriwether, Milton, Mitchell, Morgan, Monroe, Murray, Muscogee, Newton, Oglethorpe, Paulding, Peach, Pickens, Pierce, Pike,| Polk, Pulaski, Putnam, Rabun, Randolph, Richmond, Rockdale, Schley, Screven, Spalding, Stewart, Sumter, Talbot, Taliaferro, Tattnall, Taylor, Telfair, Terrell, Thomas, Towns, Troup, Twiggs, Union, Upson, Walker, Walton, Ware, Warren, Washington, Wayne, White, Whitfield, Wilkes, Wilkinson, Worth

About the Author

Gary L. Morris worked from 2009 to 2014 as a professional researcher for a major player in the genealogy field. After tracing his family lineage back to 1683, he has decided to publish these helpful guides to share the valuable information he has discovered during his career to help others trace their family lineages. An avid genealogist himself, he hopes you will find this guide factual, thorough, helpful, and most of all, effective in helping you to find your family members.